BLACK ART NOTES

EDITED AND WITH
AN INTRODUCTION
BY TOM LLOYD

THE EARLIEST AFRO-AMERICAN ARTISTS - THE CREATION OF THE
SPIRITUALS - CONSTRUCTED NEW FORMS WITH WHICH TO DEAL WITH
THEIR RACIAL EXPERIENCES. NOT HAVING BEEN SEDUCED BY THE
SCHOLASTIC MERLINS, THEY WERE FREE FROM THE MYTHS THAT
BLACK MANHOOD WAS ATTAINABLE ONLY IF ONE TRANSCENDED HIS
RACE AND GROUP EXPERIENCES.

ADDISON GAYLE, Jr.

THE WHITE MAN'S ESTABLISHMENT CONTROLS THE BLACK ARTIST
THROUGH THE MEDIA. THAT IS, THEY DETERMINE HOW MUCH
EXPOSURE THE ARTIST WILL RECEIVE. WHAT THEY DO IS TO TAKE
ONE ARTIST AND PROJECT HIM AS BEING THE BLACK VOICE. THIS
HAS BEEN HARMFUL TO OUR COMMUNITY BECAUSE NO ONE MAN CAN
CONVEY THE RICHNESS OF THE BLACK EXPERIENCE. THIS HAS ALSO
BEEN HARMFUL BECAUSE THEY HAVE MANAGED TO CONTROL THE IMAGE
THAT HAS BEEN PROJECTED.

JOHN CHANDLER

ART WAS A LIFE EXPRESSION. THERE WERE NO ART MUSEUMS OR
OPERA HOUSES IN PRE-WHITE AFRICA. ART AND AESTHETIC EXPRESSION
WERE COLLECTIVE EXPERIENCES IN WHICH ALL THE PEOPLE PARTICIPATED.
ART, IN SHORT, WAS NOT FOR ART'S SAKE, BUT FOR LIFE'S SAKE.

LERONE BENNETT, Jr.

<u>INTRODUCTION</u>

The spirit of the Black Arts Movement is expressed here by Black artists of the many disciplines embodying Black Art. Their positive philosophies affirm a need for a collective effort to project, glorify and protect Black expression from the destructive forces that threaten its survival.

What began as a counterstatement to the introduction in the catalog (herein included as an appendix) of the "Contemporary Black Artists in America" exhibition at the Whitney Museum in April 1971 has transcended its original purpose and has become more than just a rebuttal to the misrepresentations in the introduction. It has developed into <u>BLACK ART NOTES</u> which is a concrete affirmation of Black Art philosophy as interpreted by eight Black artists.

Many included are undergoing a baptism of thought; all are formulating principles and criteria as it relates to the Black aesthetic and the struggle for Black Liberation.

CONTENTS

<u>INFORMATION ABOUT THE ARTISTS</u>

MELVIN DIXON is a brilliant young writer from Wesleyan University, Middle-town, Conn. He has written many articles about Black art.

TOM LLOYD, former art instructor at Sarah Lawrence College and Cooper Union, is now organizer of community art programs. South Jamaica, N.Y.

IMAMU AMIRI BARAKA (LE ROI JONES) is one of the most respected black writers and the prime mover of the Black Arts Movement. He is Founder of Spirit House Newark, New Jersey.

JEFF DONALDSON is Chairman of the Art Department at Howard University, Washington D.C.

DAVE DAVIS is Director of Art at the Living Arts Center in Dayton, Ohio.

RAY ELKINS is Artist in Residence at Cuy Hoga Community College, Cleveland, Ohio.

FRANCIS AND VAL GRAY WARD are a husband and wife writing and research team. Val is Director of the Kuumba Workshop in Chicago, a black arts workshop of black community and creative people. Francis Ward is a correspondent in the Chicago Bureau of the Los Angeles Times.

BABATUNDE FOLAYEMI (TONY NORTHERN) has exhibited in Black communities throughout the United States and in Africa and South America. He is co-owner and director of the Harlem Art Gallery, and member of Weusi-Nyumba Ya Sanaa (House of Black Art) in Harlem.

<u>WHITE CRITIC - BLACK ART???</u>

by

<u>MELVIN DIXON</u>

        I am not about to defend the Black Arts Movement in any way, for it
needs no defense. It is indeed beautiful and artistically productive in spite
of itself. However, I would like to set the record straight about white
involvement in the Black Arts Movement, mainly criticism.
        Black Art, by definition, exists primarily for Black people. It
is an art which combines the social and political pulse of the Black community into an artistic reflection of that emotion, that spirit, that energy.
As an aesthetic foundation it seeks to step beyond the white Western framework
of American art which has enclosed and smothered any previous expression of
Blackness.
        Both by choice and design, Black art is not a part of the American
cultural scene. Its aesthetics is deeply rooted in the day to day existence
and/or activity of Black people. Any investigation of this aesthetics has
been denied or washed over so that an indigenous Black art has all but
foundered in the mainstream of commercialism.
        Black art reflects the activities of Black people. It unlocks the
ideological barriers of the slave-nigger-negro-black mentality in us to
foster a greater expression of the free creative consciousness. By definition it is beyond the sick white culture that run the entire course of its
Western aesthetics, and can now only make desperate attempts at grasping
some essence of life through a decadent nudity which only exhibits pale,
ragged, sterile bodies or forms in the name of new ART. Ha!

<u>BLACK ARTISTS</u>
        Black artists don't need that, thank God. For we have a much greater
realm to deal in .... The esoteric idiosyncrasies and nuances of Black life
are open to our fruitful investigation. And we must take full advantage of
its warmth and beauty, thereby realizing a greater artistic representation
of life.

Because we choose not to follow traditional Western approaches to art and allow its tired definitions and categories to define us, we look to life itself, our life, which as a result of cultural oppression is infinitely more different than any other life on this planet. Therein we find our aesthetics and finally our critical expertise.

And yet, the popular media of today dares to send white critics to Black shows to review some idea, some expression of art which is totally alien to their existence and their accompanying Western frame of reference.

ANGRY?

As a result of the cultural incompetence of white critics, we find such ludicrous statements like, "Black playwrights are angry" or "So and So is Black America's version of P.T. Barnum." These statements show no insight into the accomplishments of Black artists, and only degrade the quality of the work through alien references. An insult? You bet it is! When are you people ever going to stop comparing us to dead "heroes" of the Western civilization which is all but dead itself?

Attempts at such misguided comparisons show quite clearly that white America is a long way from recognizing Black people as Black people. Must we always be whitewashed, and always misunderstood?

A white person as "critic" does not belong in Black art. He cannot establish himself as one who can effectively measure the worth of Black productions for they are beyond his jurisdiction. For example in Black theatre he can't even begin to question the acting, because he has little insight into the varying characteristics and movements of Black people. It has been more convenient for the white critic to label everybody as either a "militant" or a "Tom". That hardly fulfills the responsibility of the critic in his evaluation of the success of failure of the production.

OUTSIDER

A white critic in Black art is only an outsider looking in. He cannot validly assess the artistic merit of the Black experience because, more often than not, the whole ritual is simply beyond his comprehension or concern. He is unaware of the various rhythms and pulses within the Black community, or the ideological differences among Black people. He is not in direct

communion with the artist, for Black artists speak primarily to Black people..
the Black community, and that spiritual union he is barred by necessity.

<u>AFRAID</u>
White critics cannot, or are simply afraid to, deal with the complexities of Black life styles and explore the ambivalent relations among Black people. This type of critical investigation must be the work of Black critics. It must be the commitment of the Black critic to effectively analyze the development of the varied Black arts and through a critical eye, focus towards the progress of Black art in all its dimensions.

Black art will never grow as a meaningful expression of Black people unless it is criticized by Blacks and geared in new directions with the Black community. As a member of the community, the Black critic must be a spokesman for the community and himself. He will then provide a truer assessment of the art and the artist in the move toward the liberation of Black people. White critics cannot function as such. They always stop at the "anger" and never fully and really get at the heart of the artist's message to his community/audience.

<u>FOR BLACKS</u>
All manifestations of Black art are first and foremost for Black people in an effort to liberate them to a higher level of self-consciousness. That goal has little to do with white people. So when the critics gasp at the Hollywood-ish revolution, "Uptight" and that sick, sick pseudo-militant clown show "The Lost Man", and say "Wow, look at all those angry militants, that's great" as they write in masochistic ecstasy, let the Black critics deal with the Black artists. We know what we are looking for. We know how effective Black art can be to Black people. And we deal with the situation through our own artistic and cultural frame of reference.

When white people stop trying to criticize Black accomplishments, then maybe Black artists will stop catering to the white audience for white approval. Then perhaps Black art will progress to a deeper spirituality beyond the decadent sterility of that Western omnivorous monster called "Art",..
and indeed be BLACK!

<u>BLACK ART - WHITE CULTURAL INSTITUTIONS</u>

by

<u>TOM LLOYD</u>

A focus on the institutions of the art world establishment reveals that it is one of the most deeply racist facet of our society. Its oppressive factor in frustrating Black imagery cannot simply be bypassed. Its refusal to project our unique cultural contributions separate and apart from theirs is, in effect, a total rejection of or a belief that our culture does not exist per say; for them it exists only in the expediency of its immersion into the downstream of American art.

The introduction in the catalog of the Whitney Museum is interesting. It shows how a "white culture-maker for the Black people" can skillfully use Black artists' quotes out of context and turn them into a philosophy supporting the white man's vested interests. The intrusion into the Black experience was justified by the pretension that freedom can be achieved only in the unfolding of the art for art's sake concept. Indeed can an oppressed people afford the luxury of an "undynamic" art? The answer is "no". Besides, the Black artist will never be free as long as the white man persists in playing his devil's game of picking who is to be considered free and who is to be admitted to his realm.

Indeed can the Black artists sit back and watch while white critics and white-oriented institutions dilute, polish and whitewash Black art? Again, the answer is definitely "no". And if art is indeed a creative process which involves the conscious and unconscious mind and soul, then who can assess the intrinsic value, channel and determine the growth of Black artists and critics themselves.

Black art stems from Black culture; and Black culture, inspite of all the imposition of Western culture, cannot but depart from an African source and cannot but proceed along its own line of development. A development which, in the last centuries, has been warped and mutilated but which is now seeking to shake off the trammels of oppression and to achieve its own

natural peak of progression. Inherent in such a development are conflicts
and complexities which can be understood and analyzed only by the people
involved in the struggle itself - here the struggle for a <u>POSITIVE, SELF-
AFFIRMING BLACKNESS.</u>

It goes without saying that whites, be they racist (consciously or
unconsciously) or well-intentioned liberals, cannot with any full meaning
begin to fathom the depths of Black culture. They cannot but be falsely
biased when they use their own yardstick of Western values (assumed to be
universal) to judge Black artists in terms of their own experiences. Nor
can they prevent themselves from slipping into stereotypes. Since they can
only go so far - they may see anger or other outward manifestations in the
work of the Black artists but they will never fully comprehend the life styles
of the Black people enough to enable them to get to the core of the artists'
dilemma or message to his own people.

On the other hand, white institutions which have the power to encourage
and foster Black creative energies have failed to do so. Museums have more
or less become an organ which promotes a non-art aesthetics of a Western
aesthetic in its death throes. Check out the games being played - Non-art,
Anti-art, Conceptual art, Impossible art, and Earthworks to bury all these
bizzare fantasies in. Its constant compulsion for taking an anti-life
posture shows that its artistic dynamics is ebbing out. While currently
playing the games of the white artists the institutions are programming and
pressuring Black artists to conform to the images and values of their white
audiences by giving out token rewards, white recognition and acceptance into
the art world. Consequently, some identify with their oppressors, others
tone down their aspirations and deny the relevance of their color. One wonders
to whom they wish to communicate and what do they wish to communicate? The
same might be asked of the white-oriented institutions.

Under pressure, these racist institutions make many deceptive moves -
seemingly professing reforms. In the case of museums, they hurriedly assemble
"instant token" exhibitions; always featured in these one-shot shows are the
non-political "cooperative" Negro artists whose bowing movements are readily
spotted as talent. Other institutions have gone so far as to install Negros
as trustees to give that "integrated look"; and very often they get angrier

than their white counterparts when confronted with Black demands. These
devices are used to create an illusion - an illusion that encourages confor-
mity and non-creativity. They are methods to control us through self-
denying Negros and deceptive plots to frustrate Black imagery.

Although the artist's involvement in his community must have first
priority there is still some justification to the Black artists' demand
for the portrayal of their historical and contemporary accomplishments in
established cultural institutions. Of particular concern is the Black youth
in the Public and High Schools network. Compulsory educational requirements
demand that they visit cultural institutions to view exhibitions. These
collections, however, are invariably on the history and art of cultures
other than their own. Curious minds and eyes are thus denied knowledge that
relates to their own history and culture. Also, many institutions have
educational departments which package and send out these types of exhibits
to the respective schools. Since 35% of the youth attending the New York
City Public Schools are Black this seems to be sheer ignorance or a deli-
berate conspiracy to deny a large segment of the cities youth their rightful
cultural identification.

It is evident that the cultural institutions of America have been
created for the white middle and upper classes and designed to promote only
Western ideas and culture. In this respect the Lincoln Centers and the other
major institutions should be stoned out of existence.

Black people should be aware that their money supports these racist
institutions. Cultural institutions are tax-exempt. Tax deductions are a
form of public financial support which would find their way into the public
coffers without this tax benefit. These institutions are a direct benefi-
ciary of public money - including, of course monies from Black tax-paying
citizens; they are therefore obligated to fulfill their responsibilities of
full cultural identification for _all_ citizens. As receivers of Local Assistance
Funds from the State and other public agencies their responsibilities are made
even more clear.

To ensure this representation the creation of minority-directed "Study
Centers" within major cultural institutions is an immediate "must". Its
focus would be the non-white oppressed minorities, particular consideration

being given to Black representation. The "Study Centers" should be endowed
adequate funds for a staff to conduct year-round exhibitions and programs -
independently.

  This program will correct some of the omissions and distortions of the
past and more importantly, reflect what is happening to-day in the crucible
of contemporary culture in Black and other neglected communities.

Suggestions for Study Centers in Museums and Performing Arts Institutions

1. Resources - In order to be an effective instrument of education a consistent effort must be made to acquire existing materials on the Black and
   other minority artists. The following should be acquired (by purchase,
   duplication, rental, etc.)
   a. biographies
   b. catalogs
   c. books
   d. records
   e. films
   f. critical studies
   g. slides
   h. clippings
      newspapers
      periodicals

2. Gallery space - Appropriate exhibition space for retrospective and current
   exhibitions. At least space for two exhibitions concurrently.

3. Publication of catalogs, monographs, biographical data on the artists.
   Varied levels, i.e., elementary and secondary levels.

4. Establishment of close ties with the academic community especially with
   ethnic studies programs always keeping an eye for sound publishable studies
   (theses) by scholars and experienced writers on art and culture.

5. The availability of GRANTS, COMMISSIONS, AWARDS to persons and/or groups
   of professional ability in specialized activity (art work, films, slides,etc.)

6. Liaison with appropriate departments of school systems.

7. The publication of a newsletter for the minority artists.

8. The establishment of an inter-museum program for the training of minorities in the museum profession (probably to be worked out the Metropo-
   litan Museum and the American Assn. of Museums. National in scope.
   Begin with a pilot project)

9. Cooperation with other major institutions in arranging special travel-
   ling exhibitions and performing art programs.

10. Reproduction of inexpensive art works keeping in mind children and others
    who have little money (often times none) to acquire a good reproduction.

11. Photography and the exhibition of professional photography work from
    the above named group of artists.

12. The presentation of appropriate films, i.e., those related to the program
    of the Study Center. And, where appropriate, the sponsoring of lectures,
    symposia, etc., etc.

In addition to creating "Study Centers", major cultural institutions
must decentralize, not through bureaucratic controls and administrative
programming by putting a mini-Lincoln Center or mini-Metropolitan Museum
in Harlem, but by decentralizing in a meaningful way. A way which would
provide for relevant community control in areas of planning, administration,
programming and funds.

It is also of prime consideration that Black artists should organize,
not in splinter groups that can be divided and manipulated but, under one
umbrella of common strength, conviction and purpose. Only then can effective
strategies towards a common goal be devised. Thus we must create systems
embodying a Black aesthetics that will ensure our survival, signal our
liberation and glorify our delivrance from overt oppression.

The creation of an independent <u>BLACK ARTS COUNCIL</u> which will support
and protect the interests of the Black community and its creative artists
is another "must". It could finance community cultural programs, create
Black institutions, conduct national seminars, maintain communications,

investigate and pressure cultural institutions, State Art Councils and Parks Department Councils for support.

Art, as far as possible, should be inter-connected with political and social action. Community art groups, dance workshops, storefront theatres film workshops are springing all over the country. Artists are more and more gearing and investing all or part of their creative energies in social action agencies, mental health programs, drug addiction centers and youth organizations. This turning into the community indicates a certain awareness of others in the group - something which has been previously negated. Furthermore, since many of these depend essentially on neighbourhood funding there is no requirement to support the establishment values of the dominant culture.

In a society where racist institutions are inhumane and unresponsive to the free expression of other cultures the Black aesthetic will assert itself inspite of all the obstacles of an alien culture.

COUNTER STATEMENT TO WHITNEY RITZ BROS

by

IMAMU AMIRI BARAKA

The idea that "politics," or more precisely, in the case of the Black
Artist, nationalism, is only some unnecessary adjunct to the art of the
black man, is white colonialism. Of course, the desire by black men over
the world to be Self Determining seems a bit extreme to Colonel Blimp, who
is now controller of western museums, tho his jr partner, Fagin, who used
to run a mobile pickpocketry, is now riz in many cases, to aesthete in
residence. This desire of the African Personality to reassert itself, as
itself, and very consciously, very deliberately (& as other than step &
fechit (for white desire) the 3rd stereotype in the trio), is the eruption
of a counterform in the closed field of white definition. Ethics and Aesthetics, as Wittgenstein sd, are one.

And it is too late to trot figments of white imagination, posed as
black artists, onto a scene of supposed seriousness for the concerns of
humanity, and permit them to sing their allegiance to the Western world.
The Richard Hunts and Barbara Chases & other less serious names touted as
"non-political" black artists do not actually exist in the black world at
all. They are within the tradition of white art, blackface or not. And to
try to force them on black people, as examples of what we are at our best,
is nonsensical and ugly.

Our feeling of us-ness is the beginning of our redefinition of ourselves
as us-in-the-world. Just as we must understand "personality", that is, the
special experience of a soul in the world (tho we do not accept "individualism"
the great western ethic-aesthetic which has led to the chaos of the world)
so as to speak of the black artist, the African Personality, as being
"just like everybody else" is just simply not factual. John Coltrane is a
special experience as projection of the African Personality, just as John
Cage is a special experience as projection of the special experience

that is the European Personality. True Integration in the world would be the world as a varied projection of special experiences each one refined to be hopefully beneficial in some way to the world. The personality as part of the total world community, yes, but we are not talking about the harmful "individualism" of say racism, capitalism, colonialism or imperialism.

The struggle for Self Determination is part of our actual lives, my man. The constant struggle to liberate ourselves, to raise our consciousness, to the point where we are SelfDetermining peoples is <u>an actual part of our culture</u>. The social forces and spiritual conclusions of men's lives are part of the fire that makes art. Men, including artists, reflect the context to which they owe their existence to paraphrase Maulana Karenga. But unfortunately we have always had yodelers of praise for boss even during slavery, some slaves wanted most of all to walk and talk like marssa, and denied they were even slaves, certainly they later cd not understand what they had to do with africans, or the need to liberate them, since they were just lak massa, & had only massa's concerns. "Racial hangups" indeed, one lasting racial group was called lynching, and if one definition of "highart" is that it must never depict, draw reference to or exact meaning from, the real world of living men and women, African peoples have never made much art like that before, or during slavery, or now, while we move to make our gettaway.

To paint white colored and call it black is the white man's reaction to the movement of the Black Artist for Self Determination, which is the only "artistic freedom". A Black Arts show full of whiteartists in Black face, soulpimps, pathological niggers who love white flesh, is the white man's idea of what a black arts show is all about. He is so racist he cannot understand that there is beautiful expression in the world totally unrelated to his corny little version of where beauty's at.

But in criticism of even the righteous brothers involved with all this, World Africans will never be totally liberated until we have institutions of our own to maintain and develop our own expression, and to relate that expression to the world. We must suffer the distortion of other people's imposed definitions (which is racism &/or ignorance) when we willingly or unwillingly submit to their handling and "scholarship". Wd that we wd all move to establish our own institutions and be giving up great amounts of energy towards that end. It is also one form of self-defense. They are a pyramid of revolutionary purpose. Self Determination, Self Respect (by creating institutions that express & legitimize our culture) and Self Defense- (physical mental & spiritual). Art should be about these things - It must be these things.

THE ROLE WE WANT FOR BLACK ART

by

JEFF DONALDSON

In their book <u>Black Rage</u>, brothers William H. Grier and Price M. Cobbs suggest that Black men defensively equipped with paranoic personalities survive the experience of America much better than those who are not so fortunately afflicted. And if this true, if black paranoia is a requisite for black sanity, I have no anxiety regarding my own mental health. For I feel that there forces all around me that constantly deny my humanity and even question the very fact of my existence.

These dehumanizing forces are present in every visible manifestation of the "American culture", from popular media to scholarly textbooks. If you examine a typical newspaper, you will find that Black people are only newsworthy when they are restricted, convicted, or evicted. One rarely sees a Black human-interest story, and I dare say that there are today more occurences of genuine human interest in any black community on any given day than in most white communities in a whole week. For the black community is today enjoying a rejuvenation of the spirit and a sense of belonging and becoming which is overwhelming in its goal, its tempo, and its momentum.

BLACK IMAGERY IS EXCLUDED

In my own special field, art history, I am constantly confronted with assaults on the dignity of my past and creative worth of my present and my future. I find that the art of my forebears was not art after all, but rather the intuitive expression of a people whose system of government was "tribal", whose artistic output is in the "curio" class and categorized as "primitive art", and this despite the heavy debt that modern Euro-American art owes to the work of my ancestors. Indeed, we may even lay strong claim to a sort step-parentage to classical Western art as well, since archaic Greek art sprang from the loins of Egyptian art. All this, despite the significant expression of black craftsman during the slave

period, the extensive creative output of the Negro Renaissance artists
of the 1920s and '30s, the Atlanta school of painting of the later '30s and
'40s, the outstanding black murals of the depression years, and the artistically
and socially important work done by black artists in the period since World
War 11.

ART FOR THE PEOPLE'S SAKE
Despite all these facts, the most extensive college-level reference work
on American art, published as late as 1966, makes a one-paragraph reference
to one contemporary black painter and one mulatto (that's the author's word)
carpenter of the colonial period. No other black mark stains the pages of
this scholarly ode to white supremacy, and the book is 706 pages long. Now
while my remarks have reflected the situation in art history, similar cases
could be made for black music, the black spoken and written word, black
dance, the entire spectrum of what we call the arts.
But I don't tell this in a "woe-is-me" attitude. I tell you how a
substantial number of us feel about what we see, and I tell you we don't
like it, and here are some of the things we're doing about it. Black image
makers are creating forms that define, glorify, and direct black people -
an art for the people's sake. Those of us who call ourselves artists
realize that we can no longer afford the luxury of "art for art's sake".
Black scholars are reassessing the relevance of their studies in the light
of black peoples present and future realities. We will no longer permit
so-called higher learning to separate us from our people. We will no longer
permit academic degrees to function as wedges between us and our people's
needs and desires. We will no longer permit scholarly language, useless
theoretical doubletalk, and esoteric dilettantism to make our academic and
artistic exercises unintelligible to our people. In other words, art or
knowledge that does not serve the cause of the black struggle is a waste of
valuable time and creative energy. Black artists and black scholars who do
not respond positively to the cause of black mental and physical liberation
will be considered irrelevant by their grandchildren, if I may paraphrase
brother Le Roi Jones. And as we work to define and direct ourselves, as
we respond to the challenge of black needs, you must realize, if you are
women and men of good will, that you have an equally important challenge

facing you. You must realize that race relations in this country will
never be the same as they were "in the good old days". Actions must be
taken by whites as well as blacks, if we are to remain in the same country
(and there is some question as to that). And you must realize that our
roles as blacks and whites are clearly defined.

GRADUALISM IS SUICIDAL
Universities and other institutions must not respond to our need with
gradualism, for gradualism will be foolish and perhaps nationalistically
suicidal at this moment in our history. You must not respond with tokenism
because there you only delude yourselves. You must not respond with modera-
tion because this will only make a bad situation worse, and at best will
only forestall the inevitable cataclysmic confrontation that arises from
hopeless frustration. And so for the sake of us all, if we are to remain
one nation, divided even though we may be, we must propose programs that
will immediately put right past wrongs and give directions for the future.

WE NEED A NEW AESTHETICS
In art, we are calling for the revamping of the present system of
aesthetics and a purifying of the language employed in describing art forms
of cultures which fall outside of the purview of the Creco-Roman-Renaissance
tradition. Black and white are undesirable synonyms for evil and purity.
The term primitive is inadequate for describing a nonliterate culture, and
physical beauty and excellence that are truly universal and not limited to
Europe and its cultural colonies. We insist on the inclusion of histories
of African and Afro-american art in all the universities and educational
institutions that serve black people. And these histories must be written by
black scholars and not by well-intentioned white ones.

For there is a qualitative difference between being sympathetic and
empathetic. And the emphasis I place on visual art is necessary, because
visual art expression is the most profound reflection of a culture, and
our people must become more aware of their rich cultural heritage.

<u>WHITE ART HISTORIANS - BLACK ART</u>

by

<u>BING DAVIS</u>

The Black artist to-day must not be lulled back to sleep by the white intellectual speech patterns of white art historians. It never ceases to amaze me how some people will attempt to know and understand a whole way of life that is unique to this country by 'peering into'. We all know to 'peer' reveals only the surface characteristics and does not allow one to understand the total meaning of an expression. Most white art historians view the characteristics of Black artists and their work through their own limited and fragmented experiences. The white art historians' past interpretations of the Black man's involvement in art has been more like:

White man's view of ...

BLACK : Totally negative

BLACK MAN : UNacceptable as a man

BLACK MAN'S ART : A way of personal expression foreign to the Black man unless practised in a traditional accepted style (white-oriented style)

This being the underlying negative attitudes of the majority of past white art historians, it is understandable why they are unable to identify with, dictate to regulate valid subject matter - historically placed or accurately evaluated. Most of the art of the Black man include the intellectual response that exceeds the capabilities of most white art historians due to social deficiencies.

He who stops to sort and place Black artists in pre-arranged cubes is already being passed by.

<u>REBUTTAL TO THE WHITNEY MUSEUM'S INTRODUCTION</u>

by

<u>RAY ELKINS - THE PEOPLE'S ARTIST</u>

The Curator has chosen to rap on a subject that no European can rap on. Black art is something that only a Black man can express. Racism in america has made it impossible for Blacks to do their own thing. Now we have people like him running around talking and writing on the subject of Black art and making use of the same old tricks, uncle tom's and black artists who paint things that have no real meaning to the life and death struggle of Black people.

I say <u>hell no</u> to that shit. A Black artist must build Black culture, and must be willing to give his life to make sure that all Black children have something of their own to be proud of.

Black people are being killed in the streets, and the Black artist is letting white man tell him not to paint about it. All culture and arts must flow from the People's revolution. Our artist must draw and paint pictures which will inspire our people to fight to free ourselves from the "white rope". African culture is very important. The old culture should be studied and saved so as to educate future generations of Black people.

When I see Black kids being jailed and shot I say, paint it, show it to the world. When there are no jobs for Blacks and Children are starving I say, paint it. The Black artist's job is to show all the time the unjust and inhuman treatment of Black people, not to play pussycat with some European.

We have a job to do, and with the help of Allah we can achieve our freedom. As an artist I paint - a feeling that no white man can ever dream about. Nothing is more beautiful than being Black, and being alive and a part of the great mass of Black people all over the world.

<u>THE BLACK ARTIST - HIS ROLE IN THE STRUGGLE</u>

by

<u>FRANCIS AND VAL GRAY WARD</u>

The current phase of the black liberation struggle, this newest
Black Power-Black Consciousness stage, successor to the old civil rights
movement, is, without a doubt, the most profound and meaningful period
of this century for black Americans. No period has produced such sustained
political and social militancy among blacks; no period has been such a
significant break with the old, stereotyped, white-oriented past; no period
has so emphatically validated our glorious African past, as well as our
cultural and racial beauty and life-styles. And no previous period has held
such uncertainty for the black future. In fact, never in the Afro-American
past has it ever been so convincingly uncertain whether we do in fact have
a future in the white Western world.

If black Americans decide they do have a future in the white world,
the wise prognostication would attempt a forecast no further than the next
ten years. These will be pivotal, climactic years, for it will be decided
in this decade of the 1970's whether blacks will cease to exist as a people
in this country, whether they will discover real freedom and dignity,
achieve a cordial accommodation with white people. Whether a state of
permanent hostility shall exist between white and non-white peoples in the
Western hemisphere. Whenever I talk about the future, it will be this decade
I'm referring to. It isn't safe to venture a prediction beyond that.

One fact of that future has already been settled. This concerns the
leadership, planning and execution of the liberation struggle, particularly
in this century, has centered around one man or a group of men who were
vested with charisma, strong abilities and minds, and dedication to the
cause which propelled them out front as either the spokesmen for black
people or the embodiment of their struggle.

This was true up to April 4, 1968. The shot in Memphis ended all that. In fact, the period of the "noble Negro leader" was headed for extinction anyway, for Martin Luther King, Jr., even if he had lived, would have been the last of the so-called "responsible Negro leaders and spokesmen," titles bestowed on us by white people. The period of sustained militancy and heightened struggle in which blacks have engaged the past five years has lessened the role of the old, familiar "leaders" such as King or Roy Wilkins, and increased the stature and importance of previously lesser known, but strategically placed, men and women whose major contributions to the history of the period and struggle was that they happened to be at the right place at the right time. If there is one lesson the post-civil rights period has taught us, it is that those most likely to shape the destiny of black Americans in the next decade are activists and artists, who may possess additional skills as organizers.

When discussing the black artist and his role, we must begin by dispelling the false notion that an artist is an artist, no matter what his color, and that being black imposes no special responsibility on him. Though some black performers deny it, being black does have a particular meaning to the life and work of all black people, artists included, despite instances in which black people have overcome the barriers imposed by racism and achieved a measure of personal success.

Some black artists may have adopted purely Euro-American ways, may have the greatest appreciation for Western culture and values, or have been thoroughly inculcated (brainwashed, in other words) with the white, Western viewpoint. Even so, his Western inculcation cannot wipe away the subjective sense of rhythm, timing, speech and movement that his black culture environment instilled within him. The black artist may not even be aware of the extent to which blackness has influenced him, but in critical situations, the influence will inevitably surface. To the extent that any black artist hides from or denies his African or African-American roots, his courage, honesty and dignity as an artist suffer.

How, then, does the artist react if he does admit to influences of being black? Does blackness impose special responsibilities or limitations?

If the black artist is special by virtue of color, does he have to "act black" or "think black" or somehow express his blackness in his every utterance, movement or work? The simple answer to these questions is no; his blackness will express itself, consciously or unconsciously. The crucial issue underlying these and related questions is the artist's own definition of himself and his work. The issue has been debated by black and white artists for decades, maybe longer; whether art exists for its own sake, or is there a related, higher purpose to one's art. If the artist accepts the first definition, art for art's sake, then he believes his work is its own justification and cannot be subject to any external considerations, or variations other than what he himself chooses to impose.

A second school of thought argues that art, like any other aspect of life, is influenced by the artist's own culture and background, and the current conditions of his existence. His art, therefore, must be an expression of life as sees and feels it. Therefore, a Jewish painter reared in Czarist Russia, for example, cannot help but bring the influences of his life to his canvasses. The same is true of a black American, living under the lash of white racism. What else should he be expected to reflect in his art but the feelings of a victim of racist oppression?

This realization seems logical, but did not become a distinct fact of life for black artists until the Harlem Renaissance, from 1919 to about 1931. There were good and great black artists before then but few, if any, distinguished themselves as "black" or "race" artists, preferring instead to be guided by the prevailing standards of art for art's sake.

With the coming of the Harlem Renaissance, the volume, quality and nature of black arts changed - from "mainstream American" to distinctly black art, with obvious, conscious emphasis on racial themes and pride, and with a new fusion of art with the political and social struggles of the day.

This NEW conceptualization of the role and responsibility of the
black artist has tremendous import for the black present and future.
It was no accident that Garvey-type black nationalism developed during
the 1920's as the handmaiden of the Harlem Renaissance. Similarly, it is
no accident that, in the late 1960's the cry for black liberation, black
culture and identity are inseparable, products of the same source: an
intense pride in being black. Black pride and black power are based on
the same premise:
  * All of America's institutions are racist to the core;
  * The political powerlessness of black people - best symbolized by
    their colonization in big city ghettoes - is directly related to
    the racism of the white power structure;
  * That powerlessness, a political phenomenon, has been rationalized
    by a set of theories of black inferiority,black laziness, black
    ugliness, black docility. In other words, a people with no sense
    of pride, heritage or value in being themselves;
  * These theories have been validated by a white man's history and
    social science which justify and glorify white Western culture
    and standards, and the white Western economic and political
    hegemony world-wide;
  * Black economic and political power - its theory, if not the fact -
    rest on a broad amalgam of ideas which reject the entire white
    Western interpretation of history, thereby providing the basis
    for a new politics, a new culture, a new economics and a new
    psychology of black consciousness and pride;
  * A rejection of the old history and standards which would
    redefine the meaning of black existence, past and present.

With the advent of the black power movement, the black artist
assumed a new role. The artist became the re-interpretor of the black
past, the redefiner of the black present, and the analyst of the black
future. He became a creator of a new blackness which has made the most
significant break with the past of any generation of Afro-Americans.
Since the black artist is central to the re-interpretation of the past,
he must be central to the building of a new future.

In the future, I can see the black artist fulfilling six major roles:

1. creator;
2. critic (social and artistic);
3. propagandist;
4. activist;
5. hero figure to young blacks;
6. fund-raiser.

Let's discuss each one of these.

The Blakc Artist as Creator - The artist will "do his thang" to the best of his ability and commitment. He'll continue to write, paint, act, sing, dance, photograph, play and compose. The crucial difference will be that his reasons for engaging in his art - the standards governing his involvement and the kind of art he seeks to create - will be radically different from the old ones. As has been indicated before, black art of the future won't be art for art's sake, but will be based on a new fusion with the lives and times of black people.

If an artist or writer seriously probes the lives and varying moods of black people, the material he would find would be endless. He would not have to worry about variety and being "caught in a stereotyped bag," as some critics of black artists have charged. While on the point of black artists being "stereotyped," we can't go further without laying to rest that most ancient - and preposterous criticism of black artists: that they aren't "universal." Briefly, the argument goes that black artists can't be black and universal at the same time; that, to conform to "universal" standards, black artists cannot treat black subjects exclusively but must move beyond race in their work to some mythical human (non-black) understanding.

Those who argue this point of view miss two obvious, but very essential points. First, their definition of "universal" is not that at all. It is a white, Western standard they are talking about - not one which derives its essence from a collection of thought from all over the world. Their universality is not so cosmopolitan that, say, students and critics in Japan, or Korea, India, or Ghana, Brazil or China would accept its verdicts the same as students in France, England or the United States. When the white critic talks of "universality," he means those forms, subjects and habits common to the white Western world, the United States, Great Britain, Western Europe and Australia.

What the critics ought to realize is that it is they - white Westerns - who are not universal, if we take the meaning of the word literally. The world is three-fourths non-white. How, then, do white critics and students of the arts assume the arrogance, the pure gall, to presuppose that themes drawn from the lives, culture and traditions of the world's majority are somehow not universal?

Secondly, if an artist draws his inspiration only from black people on the South Side of Chicago, is it not possible that South Side blacks are just as human and have just as much to add to the totality of the human condition as the Jews in the works of Philip Roth or Saul Bellow or the Irishmen in the works of James Joyce and Sean O'Casey? The experience portrayed is both limited and universal, if one understands it - as with any other nation's expression.

The new fusion of black art with the politics of black life does not demand that the black artist consistently, without fail, every time he creates, argue the moral superiority of anything, blackness included; nor flail away at the white man in every poem, novel, play, song or picture. There may not even have to always be conflict between "the honky" and black people. In short, blackness demands from the artist, a consistent honesty, a truth to his being, and the fulfillment to his obligation of being black. If these standards are obeyed, his range of subjects and themes will be limitless, and his universality never in question.

<u>The Black Artist as Critic</u> - This role naturally follows from being an honest, truthful creator. Black artists dealing with the realities of the black condition, and the white condition, are strong, forceful critics, indeed. One could argue that their criticism need go no further. However, it must go further. The artist must be a self-critic. The artist must be certain that his visions of life, as it is and as he would like to see it, are so accurately and clearly defined that those who view or listen to his work can share his vision. If the artist is to be crucial to the building of a new future, he has the responsibility to outline and advocate those laws, standards and values he feels are necessary to that future. The artist

must be a visionary, a social analyst, the guardian of sacred morals and traditions, the teacher, the questioner and/or foe of those people, practices or habits which do not belong to the new, revitalized blackness.

The black artist has got to perform this role consciously, not necessarily at the risk of diluting his artistic integrity or freedom. The role of the critic, consciously and zealously pursued, will allow for maximum freedom. Indeed, the area of criticism itself may well be another dimension for artistic exploration.

<u>The Artist as Propagandist</u> - This function can engage us in discussion for a lifetime. It goes right to the heart of what academic purists call non-ideological art and scholarship. Their argument is that art and scholarship must be pursued without the imposition of ideological considerations, which, if felt, will prejudice their results and jeopardize their integrity.

The non-ideological argument has essentials which, I agree, are useful to blacks. However, its application doesn't prevent black artists from fulfilling their roles of propagandists. That role comes naturally if the artist is true to his subjects as he honestly sees and feels them. Any good writer, for example, who lays bare the sickness of Western society, or the brutality of white Western man, is a good propagandist for the liberation struggle, perhaps unconsciously or unintentionally. There are legitimate limitations to this role and the artist must define his own line of demarcation between artistic fulfillment and the obligation as propagandist. Let me also point out that the liberation struggle does not demand that every single principle of Western society be jettisoned, but that it be revalued in terms of its usefulness to the struggle, and to the new black future. The crucial idea to remember is that the current status of the black condition demands the obligation be met in some way by the artist.

The black artist is morally bound to take up the cause of black liberation in his work, some perhaps more than others, but all to some degree. This assumption rests on two arguments: (1) That no black artist can be true to himself, having been born, reared and shaped by white Western (racist) institutions, without dealing with racism and, at least, by implication, the black liberation struggle. If he is to reflect those forces and values which gave him his being, his vision of the world, how can he avoid dealing with that world from his point of view and remain honest? (2) Although artistic freedom allows the artist a choice of subjects, moods and themes to treat, that freedom does not permit him to skirt the responsibility to black people and, in a larger sense, of all mankind. If there is any limitation on the artist's right to choose his medium, subjects and level of work, it is the overriding imperative of his own freedom as a person, his manhood, and the sacredness of his life as well as the lives of those he purports to explore or influence.

<u>The Black Artist as Activist</u> - The activist role has a practical as well as creative side. Practically, the black artist, like other black people, may one day have to engage himself in the struggle for sheer physical survival. He may have to pick up the gun and use it. If not that, he may be thrust into the position, at any moment in time, of being the chief planner or theorist for a particular phase of the revolutionary warfare. Even if these eventualities don't occur, the artist, from time to time, needs the exhiliration, the warmth, the education of personal contact with things happening in the street.

Creatively, if the artist is to capture the feeling and spirit of those critical movements among black people, he must be there. He must be a part of them, among and of the people doing the shooting, the burning, the dying, whatever and wherever the action is. The black artist must sometimes become a reporter, not merely a statistical recorder of deeds, but an accurate reporter and interpreter of those deeds for the sake of an accurate historical record. He may record them as part of his art. Whatever his level of commitment and methods, the black artist must be involved. For activism is a critical part of that black life which he must live, know and explore and interpret. However, it should be added that being in touch with brothers and sisters everywhere, whether they are on the corner, in the bars, in the park or direct acting in the struggle, is a critical phase of the artist's preparation for creation, and of his "re-creation" (spiritually) for further creation (artistically).

<u>The Black Artist as Hero-figure to Young Blacks</u> - This role, relatively minor now, but which will grow in importance, has not been thrust upon some

black artists. Perhaps it never will be. But it is important to discuss, however, because of the value of the artist's place in the building and shaping of the black future, and the uniqueness of the hero-figure in black life in America, especially the cities.

Outside of those image-figures young people find within their own families, the most popular hero-figures to young blacks have been athletes. Though their value to black children and as black hero-figures is grossly and dishonestly inflated by white people - particularly newsmen - the hero-figure, nevertheless, does have a place in the life of black people, if only to serve as a symbol of healthy adulthood. Black athletes, for the most part, were never the clean livers, and good Christians they were pictured to be. In real life, they were most frequently precisely the opposite.

The black artist, because of the increasing importance of his place in the emerging black communities across the land, may find himself thrust into the position of being one of the most popular, respected hero-figures by young blacks. If one examines the popularity of Ameer Baraka, or Don L. Lee, leader of a new school of militant young black poets; or of James Baldwin, Gwendolyn Brooks, Larry Neal in New York, or Gaston Neal in Washington, D.C., one would find elements of the black artist already emerging as a hero-figure. The artist, through his work and personal example of discipline, will assuredly have its positive effect on young black people.

<u>The Black Artist as Fund-raiser</u> - Most black artists have already been doing this for some time and shall continue to do it with increasing regularity. It is also part of the artist's life and commitment to black people and their struggle. The amount of time devoted to causes will vary from artist to artist. Their activities will vary, depending on their talents and time. While some painters may find themselves selling some of their works and donating the proceeds to the community museum that sponsored the art show, black poets, or actors or singers may find themselves performing, without charge, at rallies in behalf of a worthwhile cause.

The artist as fund-raiser again raises the question of whether artistic freedom is somehow threatened and/or lessened by the demands of a rising social consciousness. To those harboring such fears or doubts, a short, but timely reminder: The burgeoning social consciousness which black artists express through their efforts to sustain worthy causes through fund-raising, should not be seen as a burden on their creativity, but as an opportunity to expand their understanding of people and things via increased contacts.

What kind of future can black people expect? The uncertainty of the black future is created by the uncertainty of the white response to black demands for liberation. In the interplay of demands and response, these facts are clear: black people will settle for nothing less than total liberation, white people will concede nothing without a demand. White people, given the options of black liberation or black extermination, may choose the latter, if they are led to believe that extermination of blacks will cause them no great sacrifice, and that this is the only way to handle "the problem".

The timing of the black future will be determined by the degree to which demands for liberation are met. However, which of the two options white people choose to exercise and how soon will be left up to the black people, for the choice and exercise of either option will depend ultimately on the intensity of the black struggle, how much is demanded from whites and how soon. In this sense we blacks will ultimately determine our own future - or if we'll have one.

With the conflict clearly drawn, the future of black people in America seems to be limited to either repressions, genocide, continued hostility, racial separatism as a form of tenuous co-existence, migration to a motherland, or simply social and political stagnation - where we do little or nothing and just hope for a solution to the problems of race and class, in other words, Moynihan's "benign neglect".

Is there reason to hope for a just solution? Does a just solution seem imminent? Both answers are no, for an affirmative answer to either must be based on an honest assessment that the white power structure is changing fundamentally and accepting the inevitability of sharing power, wealth and freedom with non-whites. No such assumption can be made now, and yet it is this very change - in white people, white people with power - that must be the essence of a just, orderly and free society for blacks and whites.

If the black artist has a dilemma, it is that, despite his realization of the black burden and white responsibility, he must address himself primarily to black people at the present time. He cannot talk to the white power structure because it won't listen to him and because his primary responsibility is to black people and their plight.

The task of educating the white power structure of this country to morality and reason rests with white people, particularly white artists and teachers. For them and all well-meaning whites (whoever and wherever they are): their job is not to seek work, or understanding or chances for study among black people, but to exert their energies changing the minds and hearts of white people. Changes inside the hearts and heads of the power elite at Chase Manhattan Bank, General Motors, the Pentagon or the White House are worth far more to black people than all the changes that white missionaries could ever dream of making in Harlem, Chicago, Watts, Africa or anywhere else in the Third World.

<u>THE RE-DEFINING OF BLACK ART</u>

by

<u>BABATUNDE FOLAYEMI</u>

    At this time in history when the Black man is beginning to control
his own destiny, there is an urgent need for clarification and definition
of all those elements that will create his new life style. It is common
knowledge that, since being brought to this country, all aspects of the
Black man's life have been forceably defined for him by white america.
This is particularly true of Black Art forms. The lack of unity among
Black artists, the lack of exposure and communication between the Black
artist and the Black community, and the absence of a total cultural environment geared towards African concepts helped to kindle the distortion.
Until the early '60s, white america was able to condition the Black artists
and the Black people into believing that there were only a few Black people
creators worthy of mention. Black Art as an organized movement was thought
to be totally absurd. Therefore, white america was able to dictate to some
degree the type of visual images that would be exposed to the Black
community and to the world. However, white america's control of the art
world was emphatically opposed. Young Black artists began to join together
in the true spirit of African communalism, in order to control the direction
of their art forms. The Black artists, by purging themselves of all Western
concepts and definitions of art and by submerging themselves in the
traditional African and Eastern concepts of art, were able to re-establish
the religious and spiritual motivations that made art such an integral part
of Black culture.

    Black art has been returned to Black people, destroying, once and for
all, white america's concept of "art for art's sake". Such Black organizations as 20th Century Creators, The Weusi Artist, Afro-Cobra and others, in
detaching themselves from the white art world, were able to re-define Black
Art. Organizations of Black artists were able to awaken the visual conscience

of Black people, and create a market for Black art among Black people.
A decade ago, all this was unheard of and non-existent. Black artists in
the '60s began to break the crippling hold the white art structure had on
them. Within the last ten years, the world has become acutely aware of the
existence of a Black Arts Movement, and international publications attest
to this fact.

There is now a growing nucleus of Black artists and many independent
Black art institutions which will assure the following generations of Black
artists that there is a well-laid Black creative foundation on which they
can build. The Black Arts foundation is rooted in spiritualism and a
conscience of the Supreme Being. Therefore, the white art world's feeble
attempt to understand, control or define Black art is at best a "sad joke",
because they are trying to hold back a force that has already passed them
by. White america will never again define what is Black Art.

"Unless an artist consciously submits his talents to
the will of his God he will never know the full scope
of his creativity."

APPENDIX

THE INTRODUCTION IN THE CATALOG OF THE
"CONTEMPORARY BLACK ARTISTS IN AMERICA" EXHIBITION
AT THE WHITNEY MUSEUM, APRIL, '71

by

ROBERT DOTY, CURATOR

    This exhibition is devoted to commitment - to pictures and objects
which affirm hard work, faith, patience, imagination, and aesthetic
integrity; to creation, bringing forth life or causing life to be realized
anew; to human values, both intellectual and emotional.
    It is devoted to American artists who are black. Creative individuals,
with widely disparate intentions, ideas and goals; artists whose works are
categorized as "black art," or "Afro-American art," despite the fact that
diversity is their universal trait.
    It is devoted to concepts of self: self-awareness, self-understanding,
and self-pride - emerging attitudes which, defined by the idea "Black is
beautiful," have profound implications in the struggle for the redress of
social grievances. The black artists of Chicago's South Side painted two
civic murals entitled "The Wall of Respect" and "The Wall of Dignity," and
recently Romare Bearden wrote; "Whatever increases the self-awareness of
black people will therefore enlarge the opinion they have of themselves -
as well as the opinion other people have of them."[1]
    In his history of the Negro in the United States, *12 Million Black
Voices*, Richard Wright describes the culture of Africa: "We smelted iron,
danced, made music, and recited folk poems; we sculptured, worked in glass,
spun cotton and wool, wove baskets and cloth; we invented a medium of
exchange, mined silver and gold, made pottery and cutlery; we fashioned
tools and utensils of brass, bronze, ivory, quartz, and granite; we had
our own literature, our own system of law, religion, medicine, science, and

education; we painted in color upon rocks; we raised cattle, sheep, and goats; we planted and harvested grain - in short, centuries before the Romans ruled, we lived as men."[2]

Now, as a means of arousing greater knowledge and a desire for cultural heritage among their people, many black artists are turning to the tribal arts of Africa as a source, taking as their subject matter folklore, religious and political stories and myths, animal and other symbols, illustrations of the people, and the vivid colors and rhythmic forms of tribal artifacts. This is, in fact, a rebirth of an earlier interest in the assimilation of the arts of Africa and America.

In 1925, Dr. Alain Locke advocated that Negro artists look to the "ancestral arts" as a means of incorporating a "racial idiom" in their work. Few did, a notable exception being Aaron Douglas, who superimposed geometric motifs on his murals, "Aspects of Negro Life," in the Countee Cullen Branch of the New York Public Library. The new interest in the tribal arts stems from a desire to comprehend the beauty of exotic and traditional art and a need, both personal and public, to foster manifestations of cultural wealth. A successful conjunction of tribal material and contemporary aesthetics is found in the paintings of Joe Overstreet, whose bold color patterns are laid on canvases suspended by ropes which suggest the ancient use of animal hides. Three young artists, Ellsworth Ausby, Algernon Miller and Ernest Frazier, use color and form to create painting and sculpture which are both abstract in the contemporary mode and evocative of tribal art. The union of past and present is once again proving to be a powerful stimulus.

Commingling with the intensified development of self-awareness is a conscious effort to increase and emphasize a socio-political content. Writing in 1940, Alain Locke noted that "Much of our contemporary art is rightly an art of social analysis and criticism, touching the vital problems of religion, labor, housing, lynching, unemployment, social reconstruction, and the like."[3] Recently, Edmund B. Gaither, curator of the Museum of the National Center of Afro-American Artists, stated that "Black art is a didactic art form arising from a strong nationalistic base and characterized by its commitment to a) use the past and its heroes to inspire heroic and revolutionary ideals, and b) use recent political and social events to teach recognition, control and extermination of the 'enemy' and c) to project the future which the nation can anticipate after the struggle is won."[4] The Minister of Culture of the Black Panther Party is more explicit, commanding "all progressive artists to take up their paints and brushes in one hand and their gun in the other... bridges, buildings, electric plants, pipelines, all of the Fascist American empire must be blown up in our pictures."[5]

Such extremist exhortations are categorically dismissed by many black artists who refuse to believe that art should be subjected to the necessity of conveying a political message. They would agree with Barbara Chase-Riboud that "nobody should attempt to limit artists in their response to the world."[6] Indeed, many black artists refuse to be subjugated to collective aims. One of them is Malcolm Bailey. His drawings and paintings appertain to the iconography of black people, but in his opinion "there is no definition of black art. It is absurd to take a group of painters, whose various works and concepts differ, and categorize this group as exponents of black art just because of their skin color."[7] Writing under the title "Black is a Color," Raymond Saunders asserts: "Racial hang-ups are extraneous to art. No artist can afford to let them obscure what runs through all art - the living root and the ever-growing aesthetic record of human spiritual and intellectual experience...."[8] For artists such as these, an unfettered choice of expression is crucial, for they have realized that life offers potential freedom for the individual.

During the twentieth century, a predominant subject of the black artists has been the drama of daily life. It appears in the genre scenes of city life painted by Archibald Motley in the twenties and thirties, the portraits of heroes and leaders by Charles White, and the scenes of street life by Jacob Lawrence and Romare Bearden. Early in his career Bearden wrote: "At present it seems that by a slow study of rules and formulas the Negro artist is attempting to do something with his intellect, which he has not felt emotionally....An intense, eager devotion to present day life, to study it, to help relieve it, this is the calling of the Negro artist."[9] In the painting, sculpture and graphics of Negro artists in the thirties and forties a concern for conflict, stress, and tragedy appears constantly. Because of his personal needs and the needs of his time, the Negro artist chose realism as the chief mode of conveying his emotions and experiences. Negro art students were taught theories of "truth to nature," thus encouraging acceptance of landscape, still-life and genre subjects as suitable topics. For the black artist, realism was more than a style or technique, it was a means of communication. Charles White's portraits of leaders such as Frederick Douglass were a reminder of the role the hero played in the life of the black people. Such images were a necessity, an assurance that black people would endure.

So long as black artists are inspired to create, they will continue to testify to the "black experience," the special conditions, heritage, and emotions which delineate the life of black people. But creative drives cannot be channeled. inevitably an artist reacts to the ideas and techniques which constitute the current mode, sensing and assimilating new directions of thought and vision, or the evolution of his own technique and ideas guides him toward a new result. Richard Hunt and Barbara Chase-Riboud first received attention for their figure-oriented sculptures, but over the course of a decade both have worked toward abstraction, while retaining references to the organic in their pieces. As a young artist in California, Daniel Johnson shared a preoccupation with the value of discarded objects and produced rough assemblages which often symbolized racial conditions. Since moving to New York, Johnson has been preoccupied with problems of color, form and space. Melvin Edwards entitled an early group of welded steel pieces "Lynch Fragment Series," but his recent work is more allied to the anti-formalist trend of contemporary American sculpture. William Henderson painted a series of demonic images from the black world, but he has now refined both his technique and imagery to pursue hard-edged, geometric abstraction. The nuances of color and images of Africa are the vehicle for paintings by Frank Bowling. These six are representative of a new generation of black artists, who inherited their own culture and sought the universal canons of the visual arts. Their task will be the accommodation, or rejection, of venerable emotions and new stimulii.

Whether bitter or jubilant, the initial impetus for taking up brush a pencil, stone or metal, is often personal experience and its emotional condition. But the creative act is rarely sustained indefinitely by passion or desire. Generally the artist relies on conventions or systems, established methods and procedures for organizing the format of object or image. A rational approach to complex problems is neither convenient nor expedient for

the black artist. He must answer to his own cultural loyalties and the
community, both of which insist that he create art that expresses blackness. Nonetheless, young black artists are facing the dilemma. William
T. Williams has made an outstanding contribution to modern painting by
combining a distinctive regard for color with recent concepts of scale
and the frontal plane of the canvas. Alvin Loving also employs color on
a grand scale, constructing each painting by a system of modular units,
and John Chandler manipulates color values and spatial relations. Their
command of means is significant , but it is their ambition and integrity
which demands respect.

Ultimately the black artist and his audience must respond to "the
authority of the created thing," that unique quality which originates
only with the creative individual, and which flourishes only under a spirit
of free inquiry. The need for that freedom was never greater.

Notes

1. Romare Bearden, introduction to the exhibition <u>The Black Experience</u>. Lincoln University, 1970.
2. Richard Wright and Edwin Rosskam, <u>12 Million Black Voices</u>, New York, The Viking Press, 1941, p. 13.
3. Alain Locke, <u>The Negro in Art</u>. Washington, D.C., Associates in Negro Folk Education, 1940, p. 10.
4. Edmund B. Gaither, <u>Afro-American Artists: New York and Boston</u>, Boston, The Museum of Fine Arts, 1970.
5. Quoted by Lawrence Alloway, "Art." <u>The Nation</u>, Vol. 211, No. 12, October 19, 1970, p. 382.
6. "People: Barbara Chase-Riboud," <u>Essense</u>, Vol. I, No. 2, June 1970, p. 62.
7. "Black Art: What Is It?" <u>The Art Gallery</u>, Vol. XIII, No. 7, April 1970, p. 32.
8. Raymond Saunders, <u>Black Is a Color</u>, privately printed pamphlet, 1967.
9. Romare Bearden, quoted in Cedric Dover, <u>American Negro Art</u>, Greenwich, Conn. New York Graphic Society, 1960, p. 32.

Editor and Designer (1971): Tom Lloyd
Managing Editor (2020): Camille Crain Drummond
Managing Designer (2020): Scott Ponik
Proofreaders (2020): Allison Dubinsky and Adjua Gargi Nzinga Greaves

Primary Information
232 3rd Street, #A113
Brooklyn, NY 11215
www.primaryinformation.org

Printed at Offset Print Shop

Primary Information would like to thank Amina Baraka, the Benjamin S. Rosenthal
Library at Queens College, Jameela K. Donaldson, Willis "Bing" Davis, Cynthia
Dixon, Deanna Dixon, Babatu Gray, Danielle Johnson, Kravets Wehby Gallery, Glenn
Ligon, Carol Lloyd, the Museum of Modern Art, Marilyn Nance, Akivah Northern,
Nathaniel Otting, the Queens Public Library, Lori Salmon, the Schomburg Center
for Research in Black Culture, Val Gray Ward, and Francis Ward.

WHAT IS BLACK ART? I WOULD VENTURE TO DEFINE IT TENTATIVELY
AS THAT ART WHICH DERIVES ITS INSPIRATION AND SUSTENANCE FROM
THE STRUGGLE OF BLACK PEOPLE FOR ECONOMIC, SOCIAL AND CULTURAL
POWER; AND ART WHICH REFLECTS, CELEBRATES AND INTERPRETS THAT
STRUGGLE IN A STYLISTIC MANNER WHICH IS MEANINGFUL TO THE
AFRO-AMERICAN COMMUNITY AND MEMBERS OF OTHER OPPRESSED
MINORITIES.

HUGHIE LEE-SMITH

BLACK ART CAN BE RECOGNIZED FOR ITS WARMTH, ITS
FERTILITY, ITS VISCERAL QUALITIES.

JOHN BIGGERS

BLACK ART IS A VISUAL ATTEMPT TO FIND A VIABLE FORM
WHICH RELATES DIRECTLY TO THE BLACK EXPERIENCE. WE ARE
UNDERSTANDING IN A VERY PRECISE WAY THAT WE ARE A PEOPLE
OF A PARTICULAR RACE AND CULTURE. IT IS THE GRAPHIC
LANGUAGE OF SELF-ASSERTION AND IMMINENT MATURATION OF
BLACK PEOPLE LIVING IN A DEGRADING AND OPPRESSIVE SOCIETY
THAT OFFERS LITTLE LIBERATION OF THE BLACK POTENTIAL. IT
IS AN ATTEMPT TO IMPRESS IN BLACK TERMS THE SENSE OF WHO
AND WHAT WE WERE, WHAT WE ARE NOW, AND WHAT WE CAN BE.

PAUL KEENE

BLACK PAINTERS MUST REALIZE THAT WE, TOO, HAVE AN AESTHETIC.
WE NEED NOT NECESSARILY WAIT FOR WHITEY TO APPROVE OUR
AESTHETICS. WE HAVE A PSYCHOLOGICAL NEED: WE OURSELVES MUST
FIND SOME SALVATION. WE MUST FIND THAT IT IS NO LONGER
NECESSARY THAT WE WAIT PATIENTLY, WHILE THAT WHITE POWER-
STRUCTURE-THAT-BE DECIDES WHICH ONE OF US WILL MERIT ANY
CONSIDERATION, IF ANY, AND TO WHICH LITTLE BLACK ANTICIPATING
ARTIST THEY WILL, IF THEY SO DEIGN, GIVE ONE OUNCE OF
RECOGNITION.

BERNIE CASEY

UNLESS THE BLACK ARTIST ESTABLISHES A 'BLACK AESTHETIC'
HE WILL HAVE NO FUTURE AT ALL. TO ACCEPT THE WHITE
AESTHETIC IS TO ACCEPT AND VALIDATE A SOCIETY THAT WILL
NOT ALLOW HIM TO LIVE.

BROTHER KNIGHT